COLLEGE BY MAIL

COLLEGE BY MAIL

JO JENSEN

arco 219 Park Avenue South
New York, N.Y. 10003

Published by ARCO PUBLISHING COMPANY, INC.
219 Park Avenue South, New York, N.Y. 10003

Library of Congress Catalog Card Number: 70-184765

Paperback: ISBN 0-668-02592-1

Library Binding: ISBN 0-668-02591-3

Printed in U.S.A.

ACKNOWLEDGMENT

I would like to thank all sixty-four colleges and universities listed in this book, and the National University Extension Association (NUEA), for their helpful advice and generous offers of assistance in compiling the materials herein.

PREFACE

Sixty-four major colleges and universities in the United States currently offer opportunities for correspondence study. Each school is a member of the National University Extension Association (NUEA), which serves to protect the quality of credits earned through correspondence teaching. As a rule, credit earned is freely interchangeable among these institutions and may also be used in many colleges and universities *not* offering study opportunities by correspondence.

Whether your aim is education toward a college degree, occupational advancement, or personal growth and enjoyment, a unique opportunity is provided through correspondence study.

Whatever your particular objective, you will find correspondence study has certain advantages. It offers freedom to study at hours of your own choosing, in familiar surroundings, and at your own pace. It challenges you to provide the motivation, initiative, and self-discipline essential to all learning.

Your interest in correspondence study indicates that these are traits you have in common with thousands of students now enrolled in study-by-mail programs at prestigious colleges and universities around the United States. You are invited to join with them in the adventures of intellectual discovery, and the rewards of increased professional competence and personal growth. You will be unhindered by class requirements of time and space. You receive individual attention to an extent not possible in a large on-campus lecture class. You are limited only by your own potential.

Instructional programs have been planned to assist a cross-section of the population. Courses offered through correspondence are prepared, taught, and kept up-to-date by some of the most outstanding faculty members on the various campuses throughout the nation. And they cover the same subject matter as corresponding courses taught in residence.

If you want to finish high school, or even complete the elementary grades, then this program is certainly for you. If you want credit toward a college degree, you can earn it in this manner. Even if you already have a degree, advanced graduate credit is available. If you want a professional certificate, it is offered. And even if you simply want to learn for fun—try correspondence. It's only as far away as your mail box.

HOW TO USE THIS BOOK

This guide book will give you general information about subjects available from those universities and colleges which are affiliated with the National University Extension Association (NUEA). You are urged to read carefully the various chapters, to select three or four institutions which, according to these listings, seem to meet your requirements. Then write them for their more detailed bulletins.

1. Carefully read through the Table of Contents for an overview of the complete information contained in this book.

2. Read Chapter 1 and Chapter 2 of Part I to be sure you completely understand all of the possibilities offered through NUEA correspondence study.

3. Look through the course listings (Chapters 4 through 8) for the subjects in which you are interested. Check several possibilities. Read through each of these four chapters for variations in offerings. The courses listed may not always be by the precise title you have in mind, or under the subject you have been accustomed to. There are over four thousand courses listed herein.

4. When you have identified the various subjects you would like to take through correspondence, note the numbers of the institutions which follow each course title. Then refer to the list of all 64 NUEA schools covered in Chapter 3. You can readily identify the colleges which currently offer those particular courses.

5. Decide on three or four colleges or universities you would like to consult further. Simply write them for more detailed information, using the addresses as given. Request their current correspondence bulletin and an application form. If bulletins fail to give the information desired, do not hesitate to request additional information. Each institution will be happy to answer specific questions.

NOTE: This correspondence guide is designed to give you reference to the university or college of your choice. It is not a complete catalog of information in itself. Write to any of the correspondence study departments listed herein for further details.

CONTENTS

Preface

How to Use This Book

Part I

Part II

Part III

Part IV

COLLEGE
BY
MAIL

PART I

1

Introducing Accredited Correspondence Education

Correspondence study combines the essence of classroom work—guidance of an instructor—with the convenience of learning at home. Students prepare written assignments and submit them, along with questions they may have, to their course instructor. He then reads, corrects, and grades their work, returning it with his comments and answers to any questions raised.

Opportunities for correspondence study offer a broad range of courses taught by specialists who are members of the university or college faculty. Students from many states and a number of foreign countries enroll, and many earn credits to be applied toward a degree. Others add to their comprehension of occupational or professional skills, while still others satisfy an intellectual curiosity that motivates them to seek knowledge for its own sake. As a way of continuing education, correspondence study can not only help students gain immediate objectives but it can also broaden their personal horizons as well.

Various research studies have shown that most subjects can be taught and learned effectively by the correspondence method. The *study guide* takes the place of the classroom teacher, in part. Further teaching is done when the instructor gives his personal attention to the student's lesson report. Often a correspondence student receives more personal attention than he would if he were enrolled in a large class.

A University of Texas study shows that there is no significant difference between the achievement of high school students of comparable ability and background who took the correspondence course in physics and those who took the same subject in a regular class. Both groups used similar laboratory facilities, but only the class group met with a qualified science teacher.

North Dakota State University conducted a five-year survey of students who did many of their high school subjects by correspondence. Each year the correspondence

1

students did as well as, or a little better than, the class students in the same subjects. Furthermore, most of the correspondence students said that they were well prepared by their correspondence study.

A study at Pennsylvania State University revealed that degree candidates studying by correspondence earned somewhat higher grades than did class students in the same subjects. Furthermore, students with a genuine aptitude for a particular course tended to complete it in less time by correspondence.

Each method of instruction has its own built-in strengths and weaknesses no matter how rigorously quality is stressed. Correspondence instruction is more than a convenient alternative for those who cannot attend class; it is a choice available and useful to all. The chief value of correspondence instruction may be summarized as follows:

1. It produces a close teacher-student relationship.
2. It places an emphasis upon individual participation in a setting favorable to each student.
3. It provides an opportunity to proceed, to a large extent, at one's own pace, competing with oneself rather than with others.
4. It nurtures the development of self-discipline and good study habits essential to independent study in college and life situations.
5. It allows full participation by each student whenever faculty and student "meet together" through the correspondence assignments.
6. It provides an opportunity for a private learning environment. Besides aiding the concentration of the correspondence student, private learning encourages the freedom of thought, expression, and criticism which are often repressed in group situations.

Will the postman ring twice, leaving an intriguing package for you today? If you're one of the hundreds who enroll each day in correspondence courses, this may be your day.

What's in the package? The contents depend on the course, but usually you'll find a standard textbook, perhaps a printed workbook or laboratory manual to accompany the text, a mimeographed manual on "How to Study a Correspondence Course," some miscellaneous papers, and a study guide for the course in which you are enrolled.

Study guides vary considerably, but a good study guide has three distinct elements which frequently appear in this order: (1) the assignment to be studied in the text and/or other sources, (2) the "study notes," instructor's message, or commentary on the subject-matter of the lesson, and (3) the lesson report or written work to be submitted by you, the student.

The study notes are one of the ways in which the correspondence instructor actually teaches the course. In these notes he says what he might say in class or in a private tutoring situation. Correspondence instruction offers a one-to-one faculty-student relationship at the time the instruction takes place. From this arrangement, student and teacher often develop a close working relationship.

Your study guide, along with the other required materials furnished you, provides all the information you need in order to complete the course successfully. Thus, no matter how remote your location, you have adequate facilities to do the task at hand. Frequently, additional sources will be suggested, but these materials are in no sense required.

Your study guide often provides both a good preview and a good review of each lesson. It may restate some of the material in the text, explaining it in different words. It often includes additional information and one or more points of view not given in the text. It may raise some thought-provoking questions!

In various ways the study guide serves to get your interest. Sometimes controversy is used. At other times dialogue, analogy (a story kind of comparison) and even well-placed humor are used as teaching tools. The questions and problems in the lesson report are a challenge. They cannot be adequately answered by merely looking up something in the text. You must be able to discuss in your own words, to give reasons, to show the why as well as the what. Often you will be expected to relate what you are learning to something learned previously or to information not found in the course. You are encouraged to be observant, to be curious about what you read and see, and to think both logically and creatively. In a class you may sit back while others participate actively, but in a correspondence course you do all of every lesson.

As a student, you should strive to do your best work at all times rather than be content with merely passing a course. It will be easier for you to be at your best if you establish regular study habits and send in your lessons promptly. One lesson a week is a good average rate for a busy person with job and home responsibilities.

It might take a while for you to develop good study habits. The chances are very good that you *can* succeed as a student if you really want to. Maybe you are an adult and it has been a long time since you were a full-time student. Perhaps you were not a very good student in high school years ago. That does not mean you can't be a good student now. In fact, all 64 of the colleges and universities covered in this book believe you can if you are willing to try. As an adult, you have at least two advantages over a younger person. First, you have learned more from life. Second, you have a better realization of the rewards of study. The various institutions try to do their part. They make the courses as interesting and as useful as they can. Now you must do your part. Get started!

The faculty are experienced teachers who teach correspondence courses because they believe in this type of instruction. They are not mere paper-graders. Teaching comments are an important service provided by the faculty members. These comments are often so personalized that students feel they know the instructor even though they have never met.

Another service is prompt processing—usually. The faculties are asked to keep a student's paper no longer than a week at most. You should have your paper back in about two weeks. Remember that it must travel from you to the school's office, from the office to the instructor, back to the office, and then to you.

How long does it take to finish a course? The answer to this question depends on you. Are you a self-starter? Will you stick to a regular study schedule? How much study time do you have available each week? How efficiently can you master the work at hand?

Unfortunately some students buy the course but never get started. Others almost finish but lack the extra push that assures completion. Lack of time, increased job responsibilities, and increased home responsibilities are the usual reasons given by people who drop out of courses. But, interestingly enough, the students who finish have to cope with the same problems and often more.

As a rough guide you might plan on completing one lesson a week. Don't be too slow, or, on the other hand, don't be too fast. The slow student forgets a great deal. The fast student repeats his mistakes endlessly because he does not wait for his instructor's comments. If you begin on a regular schedule, you should receive lessons back before you have progressed too far along.

Is there a time limit for completion of a course? Yes, you usually must complete the lessons and the final examination within two years of the date of your enrollment in order to receive credit. This is a liberal time allowance—actually, it is about three times as much time as you would normally need. If you are inactive for a year or more, you will be dropped from a course. You may be reinstated within the original time limit if the course is still available, if you can resume study on a fairly regular basis, and for a small fee. The time limitation is important because, if your participation is extended over a long period of time, you will not get the full benefit of the course. Furthermore, courses change drastically over the years.

Can you enroll from a foreign country? Most courses are available to residents of the United States and Canada and to military personnel and others located overseas who are served through the American postal system (American embassies, Army Post Offices, Fleet Post Offices, etc.). Some schools do serve foreign students, those beyond the reach of the American or Canadian postal systems. It is required that foreign students read and write in English to be eligible. Check in Chapter 3 for those schools serving foreign students and overseas enrollments of other types.

Should you tell your employer? That's completely up to you. Usually employers like to know about any worthwhile achievement of an employee even if it is not directly related to the employee's present work. Many industrial firms and other organizations are willing to pay a portion of the cost of correspondence study for their employees. Some have financial arrangements of this kind directly with the college or university. Check with your employer to see if you are eligible for such assistance. If you ask a school to notify your employer of your success, they will be glad to do so.

2

General Information on Correspondence Study

Education has been one of our universal goals in America, one of the essential elements in our pursuit of happiness. Because it has not always been possible even with a broad system of public classroom education for each one of us to receive all the formal instruction we want or need, many colleges and universities have recognized a responsibility for the constant and continuing education of students beyond the reach of formal classroom programs. Many institutions include correspondence study as one of the methods of assisting students in their education programs. These programs seek to combine the teaching qualities of the academic campuses with the pioneer spirit of the individual learner, making the best possible instruction available wherever the student happens to be.

Study and learning are processes that go on within the very private realm of the individual mind. The advantages of discussion and interplay of ideas commonly attributed exclusively to the classroom need not be entirely lost to the correspondence student who may discuss his studies with family and associates in his everyday world. The independent student is not necessarily an isolated student. He is almost always a determined student and therefore a worthy student. He will usually find in correspondence study the kind of individual, independent study program he needs and wants.

CREDIT OR NON-CREDIT

Credits are the units by which academic institutions measure student performance. Basically academic credits represent the number of hours spent in class in any given school term. One high school unit represents the amount of the accomplishment expected in one year in a given subject. College quarter hours or semester hours represent the accomplishment in a given subject in one quarter or semester. The offerings which are designed to give by correspondence the equivalent of classroom units carry the same credit and are listed as *high school credit* and *college credit* courses in Chapters 4, 5, and 6.

Many courses which are offered by correspondence for special requirements do not follow any residence credit pattern and are therefore not measured in credit units. These courses may be single, isolated units complete in themselves or they may be parts of a certificate or professional sequence designed to lead the student step-by-step to an advanced position in the subject area. These are listed in Chapters 7 and 8 as *non-credit courses*.

FEES FOR STUDENTS

Educational costs vary from one institution to another. Each college or university sets its own fees for correspondence study. These fees are usually in line with regular campus course costs. They range from $7.00 to $20.00 per credit hour on the college level, and from $15.00 to $30.00 per half-unit for high school courses. Exact costs are listed in the bulletin of each institution.

COUNSELLING AND GUIDANCE

Most high schools and colleges today maintain counselling services for students in their areas. Many industries and businesses also maintain personnel counselling services. Employment agencies, both public and private, are prepared to discuss educational opportunities. Students who are uncertain about their objectives should talk with their local counsellors. Any of the schools listed in Chapter 3 will be happy to assist you in every way they possibly can.

THE NATIONAL UNIVERSITY EXTENSION ASSOCIATION

The National University Extension Association (NUEA) is the major national association of public and private institutions offering correspondence education. All colleges and universities affiliated with the NUEA are accredited by the educational accrediting agency of the state or region in which they are located. NUEA membership includes quite a number of Canadian institutions. For information covering Canadian correspondence courses, write to: Director, Department of University Extension, Queens University, Kingston, Ontario, Canada.

CREDIT TOWARD COLLEGE ENTRANCE AND DEGREES

Colleges and universities vary in regard to the amount of correspondence study work they will accept toward a degree. If you want to earn credit through correspondence study before entering or transferring to the college or university of your choice, you should:

1. Know the policies of the institution you plan to attend regarding credit for correspondence study.
2. Make sure that you are qualified to meet the admission requirements of that particular institution.
3. Select courses from this book which will fit into that institution's curriculum for the degree you are interested in.
4. Be sure to state on the application blank what specific degree you are seeking and at what college or university.

You may earn up to one half of the credit required for a Bachelor's degree at many universities and colleges through correspondence study. Degrees for work done wholly by the correspondence method are *not* granted or recognized by accredited colleges and universities, nor are such "degrees" accepted by examining boards of the different professions in the United States. The liberal chartering laws in some states permit the existence of correspondence schools whose practices amount virtually to the sale of diplomas or degrees. Such degrees have no academic value or recognition and may even discredit the professional and intellectual integrity of the holder.

CREDIT AT OTHER COLLEGES AND UNIVERSITIES

Each individual college or university determines which correspondence courses they will accept. If you want to receive college or college entrance credit at another institution for your work, you should write in advance to the registrar of that institution to be sure the correspondence courses you select will be credited. Include the complete course description in your letter. All accredited institutions listed in this book freely interchange credits for the courses covered.

CORRESPONDENCE STUDY AND THE ARMED FORCES

The United States Armed Forces Institute (USAFI) has contracted with many of the accredited schools listed in Chapter 3 for offering undergraduate college courses to military personnel. Applications for enrollment are initiated at the serviceman's base, then forwarded to USAFI, Madison, Wisconsin. Applications are reviewed at USAFI primarily to determine military eligibility. The acceptance of the application from an educational viewpoint is the prerogative of the university or college.

The serviceman or woman pays a specified enrollment fee to cover the initial costs of registration and of materials. Other costs are paid by the U.S. Department of Defense. A special USAFI plan bulletin, setting out the enrollment fees and procedures, will be sent by the *Correspondence Study Department* of any institution participating in this program. Details are also available from service education officers and directly from USAFI.

PROVISIONS FOR VETERANS

All of the college credit courses in this book have been approved by the Veterans Administration and may be taken under the provisions of *Public Law 358, Chapter 34*. However, courses taken by correspondence are *not* approved under *Public Law 634* (War Orphans Act). Apply to your regional VA office for *two* Certificates of Eligibility (VA Form 21E-1993, Sep 1966), specifying the courses or curriculum you wish to take by correspondence. When you receive your certificates, fill these out and send them to the school of your choice. The VA does not pay for textbooks. You will receive payment quarterly from the VA as you complete the assignments. When you apply for additional courses, be sure to state that you have taken previous courses under the VA program.

Keep in mind that only one change in method of study is allowed under Public Law 358. If you begin your work in residence and change to correspondence, you will not be permitted to return to residence study under the VA program. However, you may begin your course of study by correspondence and, at a later date, change to residence study. Correspondence and residence study cannot be pursued under these benefits at the same time. Write to the Veterans Administration if you want more information.

GROUP STUDY

Correspondence courses, while designed primarily for individuals, may also be adapted to the needs of reading and study groups. If you are a member of a group with common interests and objectives and you wish assistance in selecting a course or series of courses to be used as a basis for study and discussion, write to any *Correspondence Study Department* for suggestions. Include in your letter of inquiry information about the composition of the group and its motivation. This information will be important to those who will identify and recommend suitable courses, and may also determine the plan for enrollment.

AMERICAN CITIZENSHIP COURSES

The United States Department of Justice, Immigration and Naturalization Service has developed materials for citizenship study especially for candidates for American citizenship. Many of the colleges and universities listed herein are prepared to handle special registrations for correspondence study using these materials. Interested students should consult one of these institutions carrying a course in citizenship. Check Chapters 7 and 8.

HANDICAPPED STUDENTS

Correspondence study departments are especially interested in providing courses to meet the needs of physically handicapped students. The vocational rehabilitation division of many state departments of education pay the cost of fees and books for handicapped students interested in this type of study. The Hadley School for the Blind offers a number of courses from NUEA institutions with which it is affiliated. These correspondence study programs are in braille or on tape. You may write this school at 700 Elm Street, Winnetka, Illinois 60093.

SCHOLASTIC AND DISCIPLINARY STANDARDS

Correspondence students are subject to the same regulations regarding honesty in their work on assignments and examinations as are regularly enrolled students of the same college or university. A student or former student who gives unfair assistance may be penalized, as well as the one who receives it.

COURSES NOT LISTED IN THIS BOOK

If you are interested in a course not listed in this book, please feel free to write to some college or university concerning it. It may be that plans can be made to offer it. If it is not feasible to offer the course, the school will try to direct you to accredited sources from which it might possibly be obtained.

PART II

3

64 Colleges and Universities with Programs

NUMBERS FOLLOWING EACH SCHOOL LISTING

1. On the quarter hour system.
2. On the semester hour system.
3. Offers courses for elementary or junior high school credit.
4. Offers courses for high school credit.
5. Offers courses for college or university credit.
6. Offers courses for graduate credit.
7. Offers certificate programs.
8. Offers courses specifically designated as non-credit.
9. Offers courses through the United States Armed Forces Institute (USAFI).
10. Accepts and encourages overseas enrollments.
11. Accepts absolutely no overseas enrollments.
12. Accepts no overseas enrollments except for USAFI.
13. Accepts overseas enrollments for high school and college courses only.
14. Accepts overseas enrollments for college courses only.
15. Accepts overseas enrollments for college and non-credit courses only.

The National University Extension Association (NUEA) is the professional organization through which colleges and universities engaged in university extension and adult education cooperate to develop, maintain, and advance good educational practices in these service programs. It has long been recognized as one of the leading educational groups in the United States.

With the Association, those institutions which offer correspondence study courses as a part of their program comprise the *Correspondence Study Division*. The

11

administrators of those programs maintain research and study projects for the constant development of the opportunities available to their students. Most of these institutions also maintain membership in the International Council on Correspondence Education for the exchange of information and service with correspondence study programs around the world.

All the member institutions represented by NUEA are also members of their respective regional educational accrediting associations and in each instance the courses offered for degree credit by correspondence are accredited by that institution.

The National University Extension Association institutions listed herein offer a great variety of subjects and a variety of study plans on several educational levels. Those students wishing high school or college credit will find specific listings of available courses. Those students who wish information without regard to credit application have the choice of vocational, professional, certificate, or informational courses in addition to the credit courses which may also be selected for non-credit registrations.

Whether you choose National University Extension Association courses for credit or non-credit purposes, you will become a student in an accepted college educational atmosphere where good teaching is the first fundamental.

Each of the 64 schools are listed in numerical sequence. The school numbers correspond to those numbers following each course listing in Part III, Chapters 4, 5, 6, 7, and 8. Write to the school of your choice through the *Director, Correspondence Study.*

THE COLLEGES AND UNIVERSITIES

ALABAMA
1. University of Alabama   2, 4, 5, 8, 9, 13.
   P.O. Box 2987
   University, AL 35486

2. Auburn University   1, 5, 11.
   School of Education
   Auburn, AL 36830

ALASKA
3. University of Alaska   2, 5, 9, 14.
   College, AK 99701

ARIZONA
4. University of Arizona   2, 5, 14.
   Tucson, AZ 85721

ARKANSAS
5. University of Arkansas   2, 4, 5, 8, 10.
   Fayetteville, AR 72701

CALIFORNIA
6. University of California   1, 4, 5, 7, 8, 9, 10.
   Berkeley, CA 94720

COLORADO
7. University of Colorado   2, 4, 5, 7, 8, 9, 10.
   970 Aurora
   Boulder, CO 80302

DISTRICT OF COLUMBIA
8. Home Study Institute   2, 3, 4, 5, 8, 10.
   Tacoma Park
   Washington, DC 20012

FLORIDA
9. University of Florida   1, 4, 5, 7, 8, 9, 10.
   706 Seagle Building
   Gainesville, FL 32601

GEORGIA
10. University of Georgia   1, 4, 5, 8, 9, 14.
    Center for Continuing Education
    Athens, GA 30601

IDAHO
11. University of Idaho   2, 4, 5, 7, 8, 9, 10.
      Adult Education Building
      Moscow, ID 83843

ILLINOIS
12. University of Illinois   2, 4, 5, 8, 9, 10.
      104 Illini Hall
      Champaign, IL 61820

13. Loyola University   2, 5, 9, 14.
      820 N. Michigan Avenue
      Chicago, IL 60611

14. Roosevelt University   2, 5, 11.
      430 S. Michigan Avenue
      Chicago, IL 60605

INDIANA
15. Ball State University   1, 5, 10.
      Muncie, IN 47306

16. Indiana University   2, 4, 5, 7, 8, 9, 10.
      Owen Hall
      Bloomington, IN 47401

17. Indiana State University   2, 5, 9, 14.
      Division of Extended Services
      Terre Haute, IN 47809

IOWA
18. University of Iowa   2, 5, 6, 8, 9, 11.
      East Hall
      Iowa City, IA 52240

19. University of Northern Iowa   2, 5, 6, 11.
      Cedar Falls, IA 50613

KANSAS
20. University of Kansas   2, 4, 5, 6, 8, 9, 10.
      Lawrence, KS 66044

KENTUCKY
21. University of Kentucky   2, 4, 5, 8, 9, 10.
      Lexington, KY 40506

LOUISIANA
22. Louisiana State University   2, 4, 5, 7, 8, 9, 10.
169 Pleasant Hall
Baton Rouge, LA 70803

MASSACHUSETTS
23. Massachusetts Department of   2, 4, 8, 9, 11.
Education
182 Tremont Street
Boston, MA 02111

MICHIGAN
24. University of Michigan   2, 5, 7, 8, 15.
412 Maynard Street
Ann Arbor, MI 48104

25. Central Michigan University   2, 5, 14.
Mount Pleasant, MI 48858

26. Eastern Michigan University   2, 5, 14.
Ypsilanti, MI 48197

27. Northern Michigan University   2, 5, 14.
Marquette, MI 49855

28. Western Michigan University   2, 5, 11.
Division of Continuing Education
Kalamazoo, MI 49001

29. Michigan State University   1, 5, 10.
The Evening College
Kellogg Center
East Lansing, MI 48823

MINNESOTA
30. University of Minnesota   1, 4, 5, 7, 8, 9, 10.
250 Nicholson Hall
Minneapolis, MN 55455

MISSISSIPPI
31. University of Mississippi   2, 5, 9, 10.
University, MS 38677

32. University of Southern Mississippi   1, 4, 5, 9, 14.
Southern Station, Box 56
Hattisburg, MS 39401

33. Mississippi State University   2, 4, 5, 9, 13.
P.O. Box 5247
State College, MS 39762

MISSOURI
34. University of Missouri   2, 4, 5, 6, 8, 9, 10.
Columbia, MO 65201

NEBRASKA
35. University of Nebraska   2, 4, 5, 6, 8, 9, 10.
University Extension Division
Lincoln, NB 68508

NEVADA
36. University of Nevada   2, 5, 8, 9, 15.
Reno, NV 89507

NEW MEXICO
37. University of New Mexico   2, 4, 5, 9, 13.
Albuquerque, NM 87106

NEW YORK
38. State University of New York   2, 5, 6, 7, 8, 14.
30 Russell Road
Albany, NY 12206

39. State University of New York   2, 5, 14.
1400 Washington Avenue
Albany, NY 12203

NORTH CAROLINA
40. University of North Carolina   2, 5, 7, 8, 9, 10.
University Extension Division
Chapel Hill, NC 27514

41. North Carolina State University   2, 5, 8, 14.
P.O. Box 5125
Raleigh, NC 27607

NORTH DAKOTA
42. University of North Dakota   2, 5, 9, 14.
Grand Forks, ND 58201

43. North Dakota State University   2, 4, 10.
State University Station
Fargo, ND 58102

OHIO
44. Ohio University   1, 5, 9, 14.
     Athens, OH 45701

OKLAHOMA
45. University of Oklahoma   2, 4, 5, 6, 8, 9, 10.
     1700 Asp Avenue
     Norman, OK 73069

46. Oklahoma State University   2, 4, 5, 9, 12.
     Stillwater, OK 74074

OREGON
47. Oregon State System of Higher   1, 4, 5, 7, 8, 9, 10.
     Education
     1724 Moss Street
     Eugene, OR 97403

PENNSYLVANIA
48. Pennsylvania State University   2, 4, 5, 8, 9, 12.
     3 Shields Building
     University Park, PA 16802

SOUTH CAROLINA
49. University of South Carolina   2, 4, 5, 15.
     College of General Studies
     Columbia, SC 29208

SOUTH DAKOTA
50. University of South Dakota   2, 4, 5, 13.
     Vermillion, SD 57069

TENNESSEE
51. University of Tennessee   1, 4, 5, 7, 8, 9, 10.
     Division of Continuing Education
     Knoxville, TN 37916

TEXAS
52. University of Texas at Austin   2, 4, 5, 8, 9, 10.
     Austin, TX 78712

53. Southern Methodist University   2, 5, 9, 10.
     Dallas, TX 75222

54. Texas Tech University   2, 4, 5, 9, 13.
     Division of Continuing Education
     Lubbock, TX 79409

UTAH
55. University of Utah   1, 4, 5, 7, 8, 9, 10.
P.O. Box 200
Salt Lake City, UT 84110

56. Utah State University   1, 4, 5, 9, 13.
Logan, UT 84321

57. Brigham Young University   2, 4, 5, 8, 9, 10.
Provo, UT 84601

VIRGINIA
58. University of Virginia   2, 5, 8, 14.
School of General Studies
Madison Hall
Charlottesville, VA 22903

WASHINGTON
59. University of Washington   1, 4, 5, 9, 15.
Lewis Hall
Seattle, WA 98105

60. Washington State University   2, 4, 5, 7, 8, 9, 10.
General Extension Services
Pullman, WA 99163

61. Central Washington State College   1, 5, 8, 14.
Ellensburg, WA 98926

62. Western Washington State College   1, 5, 9, 11.
Bellingham, WA 98225

WISCONSIN
63. University of Wisconsin   2, 4, 5, 7, 8, 9, 10.
227 Extension Building
Madison, WI 53706

WYOMING
64. University of Wyoming   2, 4, 5, 8, 9, 13.
P.O. Box 3294
University Station
Laramie, WY 82070

PART III

4

Elementary and High School Courses

One accredited institution in the United States offers special courses for those persons who need elementary and junior high school credit. A great number of accredited colleges and universities, however, do offer a very broad range of high school courses.

These many courses are specifically designed for those students, who, for whatever the reason, cannot attend high school in the normal manner. And they are made available for high school students who cannot get a desired course at the school they attend. Credit for these courses is generally awarded through the local high school, or a state board of education.

Any student who wishes to receive credit for correspondence study, and to apply these credits toward a high school diploma, must get the courses approved *before* enrolling in any institution. Only the high school principal, a counselor, or local school official can properly do this.

Refer to Part II, Chapter 3, for the names and addresses of the institutions which correspond to the numbers following each course offering noted below.

ELEMENTARY TO HIGH SCHOOL CREDIT COURSES

ALL ELEMENTARY GRADES 8.
JUNIOR HIGH SCHOOL   8.

HIGH SCHOOL

AERONAUTICS   35, 43, 49.
ART   6, 7, 20, 23, 34, 35, 43, 45, 47, 50, 55, 57, 63.
BLACK STUDIES   20.
BUSINESS
    Accounting   21, 48, 50.
    Advertising   51, 54.
    Bookkeeping   5, 6, 7, 8, 9, 10, 11, 16, 20, 22, 23, 30, 32, 34, 35, 43, 45, 47, 48, 49, 51, 52, 54, 57, 63, 64.
    Business Correspondence   1, 6, 10, 16, 21, 23, 32, 33, 35, 45, 50, 63, 64.
    Business English   55.
    Business Law   6, 16, 21, 23, 35, 43, 45, 46, 48, 50, 51, 54, 57.
    Business Mathematics   1, 6, 7, 9, 16, 21, 23, 32, 43, 45, 50, 51, 52, 54.
    Clerical Practice   51.
    General Business   1, 6, 7, 10, 21, 30, 32, 33, 34, 35, 43, 45, 48, 50, 51, 54, 63, 64.
    Salesmanship   6, 35, 50, 51, 54, 63.
DRIVER EDUCATION   6, 35, 43, 48, 51, 54.
ECONOMICS
    General Economics   1, 5, 6, 7, 10, 16, 20, 21, 23, 32, 33, 35, 43, 45, 46, 49, 50, 51, 52, 54, 55, 60, 63.
    Modern Economic Functions   20.
ENGLISH
    Advanced Placement   10, 35, 51.
    Developmental English   51.
    Drama   6, 7, 10, 20, 35, 43.
    English Composition   6, 7, 8, 10, 11, 16, 20, 35, 50, 51, 52, 60, 63, 64.
    General English
        Freshman English   1, 5, 6, 7, 8, 9, 10, 11, 16, 20, 21, 23, 30, 32, 33, 34, 35, 43, 45, 46, 47, 48, 49, 50, 51, 52, 54, 57, 60, 63, 64.
        Sophomore English   1, 5, 6, 7, 8, 9, 10, 11, 16, 20, 21, 23, 30, 32, 33, 34, 35, 43, 45, 46, 47, 48, 49, 50, 51, 52, 54, 57, 60, 63, 64.
        Junior English   1, 5, 6, 7, 8, 9, 10, 11, 16, 20, 21, 23, 30, 32, 33, 34, 35, 43, 45, 46, 47, 48, 49, 50, 51, 52, 54, 57, 60, 63, 64.
        Senior English   1, 5, 6, 7, 8, 9, 10, 11, 16, 20, 21, 23, 30, 32, 33, 34, 35, 43, 45, 46, 47, 48, 49, 50, 51, 52, 54, 57, 60, 63, 64.

Personal and Social   35.
Textiles   16.
LANGUAGES
French
    One year   20.
    Two years   1, 8, 10, 16, 21, 30, 32, 34, 43, 45, 48, 49, 51, 52, 64.
    Three years   6, 23, 35, 50.
    Four years   63.
German
    One year   20, 21, 57, 64.
    Two years   1, 8, 34, 43, 45, 48, 51, 52.
    Three years   6, 10, 23, 30, 35, 50.
    Four years   63.
Greek   21, 63.
Hebrew   63.
Italian   63.
Latin
    One year   8.
    Two years   1, 5, 30, 45, 47, 49, 52, 54.
    Three years   6, 10, 16, 20, 35, 43, 50.
    Four years   21, 23, 34, 51, 63.
Norwegian   30, 43, 63.
Portuguese   63.
Russian   6, 30, 35, 43, 51, 63.
Spanish
    One year   5, 21, 30, 57.
    Two years   1, 7, 8, 20, 23, 32, 34, 43, 45, 47, 48, 49, 51, 52, 64.
    Three years   6, 10, 35, 50.
    Four years   63.
Swedish   30.
LIBRARY SCIENCE   63.
LITERATURE
Contemporary Literature   7, 11, 35, 50, 51.
Epic Tradition in Literature   20.
General Literature   5, 11, 16, 20, 21, 30, 35, 45, 51, 52, 56, 60, 63.
Mythology   20.
Novel
    General Novel   6, 7, 21, 35, 50.
    Nineteenth Century French Novel   20.
    Twentieth Century American Novel   20.
Oriental Literature   20.

STUDY SKILLS   7.
VOCATIONAL TRAINING
    Arc Welding   35, 43.
    Automotive Mechanics   23, 35, 43, 50, 63.
    Basic Electricity and Electronics   7.
    Beginning Woodwork   35.
    Civil Engineering   63.
    Drawing and Drafting   5, 6, 7, 16, 34, 35, 43, 45, 47, 50, 51, 63.
    Electricity, Radio, Television   6, 35, 43, 50, 63.
    Home Mechanics   35.
    Home Wiring   43.
    Photography   6, 35, 43, 64.
    Plumbing   35.
    Radio   35, 43, 50.
    Roof Framing   35.
    Service Station Management   35.
    Television   35.
WRITING
    Creative Writing   20, 45.
    Journalism   32, 35, 45, 50, 57, 63.
    Remedial Writing   30.
    Short Story Writing   6, 7, 10, 20, 35, 45, 50.

5

College Level Courses—Undergraduate Credit

Many colleges and universities offer a vast variety of undergraduate correspondence courses. Such convenient study programs are open to all adults and students without reference to previous educational background. Applications are accepted without entrance examinations. Some of the courses require certain other prerequisite study or experience. This is indicated in the individual institution's correspondence program bulletin, or in their general catalog.

The undergraduate courses listed in this chapter are available at the present time. Refer to Part II, Chapter 3, for the names and addresses of the institutions which correspond to the numbers following each course offering noted below.

UNDERGRADUATE CREDIT COURSES

ACCOUNTING

    Administrative Accounting   31.

    Advanced Accounting   6, 16, 21, 22, 45, 49, 51, 52, 54, 64.

    Auditing and Budgeting   1, 6, 22, 30, 42, 44, 51, 53, 54.

    Cost Accounting   1, 6, 7, 8, 12, 14, 16, 20, 21, 22, 31, 33, 34, 38, 42, 44, 45, 46, 47, 48, 49, 51, 52, 53, 54, 56, 57.

    C.P.A. Review   16, 55.

    Elementary Accounting   1, 3, 4, 5, 6, 7, 8, 9, 10, 11, 12, 13, 14, 15, 16, 17, 18, 20, 21, 22, 24, 25, 30, 31, 32, 33, 34, 35, 36, 37, 38, 39, 40, 42, 44, 45, 46, 47, 48, 49, 50, 51, 52, 53, 54, 55, 56, 57, 58, 59, 60, 61, 64.

    Financial Statement Analysis   6, 16, 51, 54.

    Government and Institutions   1, 6, 9, 12, 16, 22, 49, 51, 54.

    Hospital Accounting   16.

    Intermediate Accounting   1, 6, 7, 9, 11, 12, 13, 16, 20, 21, 22, 30, 34, 38, 39, 44, 45, 48, 49, 51, 52, 53, 54, 55, 57.

    Management Accounting   55.

    Special Accounts   6, 16.

    Theory of Accounting   22, 51, 53.

AGRICULTURE

    Agronomy   9, 21, 35, 60.

    Animal Nutrition   64.

    Beekeeping   30, 34, 35, 56.

    Crop Production   47.

    Dairy Farming Practices   4, 9, 22, 46, 56, 57, 64.

    Economics of Farming   5, 9, 10, 11, 20, 21, 51, 54, 56, 57, 60, 63.

    Entomology   10, 34, 46, 60, 64.

    Farm Accounts   30, 35, 51.

    Farm Buildings   34.

    Farm Cooperatives   22, 42, 51, 60, 63.

    Farm Extension Service   11, 56.

    Farm Financing   51, 56.

    Farm Products

        Forage and Field Crops   9, 10, 34, 56, 64.

        Fruit   9, 34, 56.

        Vegetables   9, 34, 46, 56, 60.

    Feeds and Feeding   10, 21, 46, 56, 64.

    Fertilizers   10.

    Forestry   9, 10, 21, 25, 30, 46, 56, 64.

    Gardening   30.

Financial Management   6, 7, 17, 21, 30, 45, 55, 57.
Fundamentals of Finance   30.
Investments and Securities   1, 6, 10, 11, 21, 22, 30, 34, 46, 55, 59, 61, 64.
Mathematics of Finance   34.
International Business   59.
Introduction to Business   16, 19, 22, 25, 32, 35, 48, 49, 59, 60, 62.
Investment Mathematics   30.
Management and Organization
Business Management   1, 4, 5, 6, 7, 9, 10, 16, 18, 22, 32, 35, 38, 45, 52, 55, 64.
Electronic Data Processing   35.
Human Relations   6, 22, 30, 35.
Industrial Management   5, 6, 7, 12, 16, 30, 36, 41, 48, 51, 52, 53, 58, 64.
Job Analysis   35, 53.
Leadership in Management   6.
Personnel Selection   1, 6, 7, 9, 12, 18, 20, 22, 35, 36, 41, 44, 47, 51, 52, 53, 55, 58.
Plant Layout   30.
Production Analysis   5.
Production Management   6, 7, 22, 30.
Small Business Management   10, 30.
Supervisory Management   55.
Theory of Business Policy   6, 22.
Marketing Practices
Advertising   1, 6, 9, 12, 22, 31, 36, 42, 44, 45, 55, 57, 59.
Consumer Behavior Science   22, 51.
Cooperatives   42.
Credit and Collection   9, 31, 54.
Industrial Marketing   22.
Institutional Marketing   18, 42.
Marketing Analysis   42, 46, 51.
Marketing Distribution   45.
Marketing Management   21, 22, 38, 51, 57, 59.
Marketing Promotion   18, 22.
Marketing Research   1, 22.
Marketing Transportation   1, 6, 16, 45, 51, 59.
Principles of Marketing   1, 6, 9, 10, 12, 14, 18, 20, 22, 31, 32, 33, 34, 38, 42, 44, 45, 46, 51, 52, 54, 55, 56, 57, 58, 59, 63, 64.
Purchasing   6, 45, 63.
Retailing Management   1, 9, 10, 18, 22, 31, 33, 42, 45, 47, 55.
Salesmanship   3, 14, 30, 31, 38, 42, 45, 55.

Special Education   16, 17, 18, 20, 28, 31, 34, 36, 40, 55, 56, 57, 61, 63.

Speech for Teachers   45, 46, 56.

Teaching Accounting and Bookkeeping   21.

Tests and Measurements   4, 5, 12, 13, 16, 17, 18, 19, 20, 21, 22, 25, 30, 32, 35, 38, 45, 46, 47, 51, 53, 55, 57, 61, 62, 64.

Vocational, Industrial, and Distributive Education   2, 4, 5, 9, 11, 17, 18, 19, 22, 28, 33, 41, 46, 51, 59.

EDUCATIONAL METHODS

Elementary Level

Fine Arts

Art   7, 16, 22, 34, 45, 50, 55, 57, 63.

Children's Literature   5, 6, 7, 9, 11, 16, 20, 27, 32, 33, 37, 40, 45, 46, 47, 54, 55, 61, 63, 64.

Music   55.

General Educational Methods

General   6, 8, 12, 18, 36, 45, 55, 56.

Geography   50.

Penmanship   9.

Remedial Instruction   45.

Science   5, 6, 7, 10, 18, 19, 31, 33, 35, 40, 50, 55, 59, 62.

Social Studies   6, 8, 9, 10, 18, 19, 31, 32, 33, 35, 45, 46, 50, 56, 61, 63.

Speech   45, 56.

Health and Physical Education   2, 5, 6, 11, 18, 20, 22, 26, 30, 31, 33, 37, 44, 45, 46, 48, 50, 52, 55, 57.

Language

Language Arts   4, 5, 6, 10, 11, 13, 17, 18, 33, 45, 46, 47, 55, 61.

Spanish   6, 20.

Mathematics

Geometry for Elementary Teachers   34.

Mathematics in General   5, 6, 8, 9, 10, 11, 12, 13, 16, 18, 30, 32, 33, 37, 40, 45, 46, 47, 55, 56, 57, 58, 64.

Modern Mathematics   6, 8, 13, 18, 19, 20, 25, 34, 44, 45, 46, 50, 57, 58, 59, 61.

Reading Skills

General Reading   5, 6, 8, 9, 10, 11, 12, 13, 17, 18, 31, 33, 35, 37, 45, 46, 47, 55, 56, 58, 59, 61.

Use of Books and Libraries   55, 56.

High School Level

Fine Arts

Art   34, 45, 55.

Music   35, 55.

Basic   1, 2, 3, 4, 5, 6, 7, 8, 9, 10, 12, 13, 16, 17, 18, 19, 20, 21, 22, 24, 25, 26, 30, 31, 32, 33, 34, 35, 37, 38, 40, 41, 42, 44, 45, 46, 47, 48, 49, 50, 51, 52, 54, 55, 56, 57, 58, 59, 60, 63, 64.
For Teachers   16, 18, 40, 45, 48, 58.
Intermediate   60.
Review   7, 18, 40, 45, 46, 47, 48, 51, 52, 57.
English for Foreign Students   6.
English Phonetics   15.
English Semantics   49.
Freshman Reading   28.
History of the English Language   9, 16, 37, 45, 51, 59, 61.
Medical English   2.
Syntax   7, 19, 51, 61, 63.
Vocabulary Building   5, 7, 36, 55, 56, 57.

GEOGRAPHY
Climatology   21, 51.
Conservation of Natural Resources   5, 9, 17, 26, 30, 34, 45, 46, 51, 52, 55, 56, 57, 62, 63.
Cultural Geography   10, 15, 44, 55.
Earth Science   10.
Economic Geography   1, 2, 4, 5, 9, 10, 11, 17, 18, 21, 24, 32, 34, 42, 44, 45, 46, 51, 52, 57, 59, 60, 63.
Human Geography   22, 31, 44, 45, 60, 62.
Introduction to Geography   2, 5, 14, 16, 17, 18, 20, 21, 22, 27, 33, 35, 40, 46, 47, 51, 55, 57, 64.
Manufacturing and Commerce   18.
Physical Geography   1, 12, 15, 16, 18, 20, 21, 24, 34, 35, 41, 44, 45, 46, 52, 62, 63.
Political Geography   17, 19.
Regional Geography
Afro-Asia Geography   52.
Anglo-American Geography   15.
Asia Geography   6, 21, 28, 35, 51, 56, 63.
Caribbean Geography   9.
Eastern Hemisphere Geography   53.
European Geography   1, 9, 15, 21, 35, 56, 57, 63.
Latin American Geography   9, 21, 27, 30, 51, 56, 57, 63.
North American Geography   1, 5, 9, 15, 17, 24, 26, 30, 32, 34, 40, 45, 46, 47, 51, 53, 54, 56, 57, 62, 63.
Pacific Northwest Geography   47, 62.
Regional Geography   15.

South American Geography   17.
Soviet Union Geography   47, 51, 52.
United States and Canada Geography   18, 35, 38.
Western Hemisphere Geography   53.
State Geography   6, 9, 21, 26, 30, 35, 38.
Urban Geography   6, 18, 59.
World Geography   1, 4, 5, 8, 10, 15, 17, 18, 19, 21, 26, 32, 34, 35, 36, 42, 45, 51, 52, 57.

HEALTH AND HYGIENE
Child Care   32.
Communicable Disease   21, 47, 56.
Community Health and Hygiene   2, 4, 7, 8, 16, 20, 22, 30, 31, 32, 34, 35, 37, 44, 47, 52, 56, 57, 64.
Elements of Health and Hygiene   35.
Emergency Health Measures   35.
Family Health and Hygiene   45.
First Aid and Safety   4, 17, 35, 37, 44, 56, 57.
Nursing   35, 55.
Personal Hygiene   1, 2, 5, 8, 12, 16, 17, 20, 21, 30, 31, 32, 33, 35, 42, 44, 47, 49, 53, 55, 56, 57.
Public Health   7, 11, 33, 45, 49, 56, 57, 61.
School Hygiene   7, 31, 35, 49, 55, 56, 61.

HISTORY
African History   6, 10, 16, 19, 31.
American History
　　　Black America   7, 21, 63.
　　　Civil War Period   10, 20.
　　　Colonial Period   7, 9, 15, 16, 21, 22, 34, 42, 56, 57, 58, 61.
　　　Constitutional History   12, 21, 57.
　　　Cultural History   10.
　　　Diplomatic History   5, 7, 9, 10, 13, 19, 30, 31, 34, 40, 45, 55, 57, 63.
　　　Early American Period (1783–1828)   20.
　　　Intellectual History   6, 10.
　　　Military and Naval History   1.
　　　Pacific Northwest History   47, 59, 60.
　　　Revolutionary History   22, 25, 34, 61.
　　　Southern History   2, 9, 10, 21, 22, 34, 46, 49, 50, 51, 56.
　　　State History   2, 3, 6, 7, 9, 10, 15, 16, 19, 20, 21, 22, 26, 28, 30, 34, 35, 36, 37, 40, 41, 44, 46, 48, 49, 51, 53, 54, 55, 57, 61, 62, 63, 64.
　　　Survey of American History   1, 2, 3, 4, 5, 6, 7, 8, 9, 10, 11, 12, 13, 15, 16, 17, 18, 19, 20, 21, 22, 26, 27, 28, 30, 31, 32, 33, 34, 35, 36, 37, 38, 40,

41, 42, 44, 45, 46, 47, 48, 49, 50, 51, 52, 54, 55, 56, 57, 58, 60, 62, 63, 64.

Twentieth Century American History   10, 13, 15, 18, 19, 21, 22, 34, 41, 53, 55, 56, 63.

United States History   18, 28.

Urban Society in America   63.

Western American History   1, 2, 3, 6, 9, 16, 25, 26, 30, 47, 50, 55, 57, 62.

Ancient History

Classical and Medieval History   10, 35, 45, 55.

Greek History   1, 10, 21, 26, 30, 42, 51, 55, 57, 63.

History of Israel   34.

History of Rome   1, 10, 21, 26, 30, 42, 51, 55, 63.

Survey of Ancient History   25, 26, 30, 40, 42, 45, 48, 49, 50, 51, 63.

Canadian History   21.

Caribbean History   10.

Church History   1, 8, 13.

Contemporary Affairs and Today's World   1, 20, 25, 49, 56, 63.

Early Modern History   55.

English History   1, 4, 10, 11, 21, 25, 30, 31, 32, 34, 36, 40, 45, 50, 51, 52, 55, 57, 63.

European History

Absolutism and Enlightenment   10.

European History Since 1500   1, 2, 6, 8, 10, 12, 13, 19, 21, 25, 26, 27, 30, 31, 34, 35, 40, 42, 45, 48, 50, 52, 53, 58, 63.

European History Since 1800   60, 63.

French History   1, 10, 13, 21, 34, 42, 57, 63.

German History   1, 34, 36r, 57.

Intellectual History   6, 10.

Medieval Europe   6, 9, 10, 12, 18, 19, 24, 40, 42, 45, 48, 51, 52, 57, 63.

Renaissance and Reformation Period   6, 10, 15, 21, 24, 34, 51, 53, 56, 57.

Survey of Western Civilization   1, 5, 6, 7, 8, 9, 10, 11, 13, 14, 15, 16, 18, 21, 25, 26, 27, 32, 33, 34, 36, 37, 38, 40, 41, 42, 44, 45, 47, 48, 49, 50, 51, 52, 53, 54, 55, 57, 58, 62, 63, 64.

1870–1914 Europe   10, 14, 18, 25, 26, 30, 41, 42, 45, 50, 56, 63.

Twentieth Century Europe   7, 8, 10, 13, 15, 18, 19, 22, 24, 26, 30, 34, 40, 42, 56, 62.

History of Eastern Cultures

Asian History   8, 30, 56, 57.

Far Eastern History   7, 26, 36, 45, 47, 57.

Near Eastern History   30.

    Reading French   1, 4, 6, 12, 13, 18, 20, 21, 22, 34, 36, 45, 49, 51, 52, 53, 57, 59, 63.

German
    Advanced German   1, 6, 20, 22, 34, 35, 36, 40, 50, 51, 52, 57, 63, 64.
    Beginning German   1, 4, 5, 6r, 9, 12, 20r, 21, 22r, 30r, 31r, 34, 35r, 36r, 37, 38, 40r, 41, 45, 47, 50, 51, 52, 59r, 60r, 63r, 64.
    Composition   20, 30, 63.
    German Drama   6, 20, 30, 40, 63.
    Intermediate French   1, 4, 6, 8, 12, 13, 16, 20, 21, 22, 30r, 31, 34, 35, 36, 37, 38, 40, 45, 49, 50, 51, 52, 53, 57, 59, 63.
    Medical or Scientific French   1, 20, 21, 31, 44, 45, 50, 51, 59, 63.
    Reading French   4, 5, 6, 16, 20, 21, 22, 30, 34, 35, 36, 40, 42, 45, 49, 51, 52, 57, 59, 63.

Greek
    Greek Derivatives   10, 30, 45, 50, 63.
    Greek Grammar   6, 8, 12, 13, 18, 21, 28, 30, 44, 45, 52, 63.
    Greek Literature   13, 21, 50, 52, 63.
    Medical Greek   21.
    New Testament Greek   52, 63.

Hebrew
    Beginning Hebrew   63.
    Hebrew Literature and Culture   63.

Icelandic   6.

Italian
    Italian Grammar   6r, 12, 13, 20, 22, 34, 36r, 45, 52, 59r, 63r.
    Italian Literature   13, 20, 31r, 36, 52.

Japanese   30r, 45.

Latin
    Latin Composition   20.
    Latin Derivatives   10.
    Latin Grammar   1, 6, 10, 12, 13, 16, 17, 18, 20, 21, 22, 30, 31, 34, 35, 37, 40r, 42, 44, 45, 50, 51, 52, 63r.
    Latin Literature   6, 10, 12, 13, 17, 18, 20, 21, 22, 30, 31, 34, 35, 40, 42, 44, 45, 50, 51, 52, 63.

Linguistics
    Introduction to Linguistics   9, 16, 51.

Norwegian
    Beginning Norwegian   30, 42r, 59r, 63r.
    Reading Norwegian   59.

Polish   30r.

Portuguese
    Beginning Portuguese   6, 34, 52, 57, 59r, 63r.
    Portuguese Literature   57.
    Reading Portuguese   57.
Russian
    Beginning Russian   6r, 12, 30, 31, 35r, 36r, 40r, 45, 51r, 52, 63r.
    Scientific Russian   30.
Serbo-Croatian   30r.
Spanish
    Advanced Spanish   1, 4, 12, 13, 20, 22, 30, 34, 36, 37, 40, 45, 49, 50, 51, 52, 57, 59, 64.
    Beginning Spanish   1r, 4, 5, 6, 12, 13, 16r, 18r, 20, 21, 22r, 30r, 34, 35r, 36r, 37, 41, 42r, 45, 47, 50, 52r, 59r, 60r, 63r, 64.
    Commercial Spanish   4, 20, 30, 50.
    Composition   30, 34, 45, 63.
    Intermediate Spanish   1, 4, 5, 6, 8, 12, 13, 16r, 17, 18, 20, 21, 22, 31, 35r, 36, 37, 40, 45, 48r, 49, 50, 52, 53, 57, 59, 63.
    Latin-American Culture   30.
    Modern Teaching for Spanish   6, 7.
    Reading Spanish   1, 4, 12, 13, 17, 18, 20, 21, 22, 30, 34, 36, 37, 40, 45, 49, 50, 51, 52, 57, 59, 63.
    Spanish Grammar For Teachers   13, 20.
    Spanish Grammar Review   59.
Swedish
    Beginning Swedish   6r, 21, 30r, 59.
    Reading Swedish   59.

LAW
    Admiralty Law   38.
    Business Law   4, 5, 6, 9, 10, 11, 13, 14, 16, 19, 22, 25, 30, 32, 33, 35, 38, 41, 42, 44, 45, 46, 48, 51, 52, 53, 54, 55, 59, 60, 64.
    C.P.A. Law Review   53.
    Farm Law   54, 57.

LIBRARY SCIENCE
    Biographical Sources   13, 56.
    Children's Books and Materials   7, 40, 45, 51, 56, 64.
    Library Cataloging   30, 34, 55.
    Library Fundamentals   37.
    Library Work with Children   55.
    Practical Library Science   13, 30, 34, 55, 56, 64.
    Public Library   13, 55, 56.

Italian Literature   20.
Literary Criticism   45.
Medieval Literature   7.
Mythology   1, 6, 21, 34, 50, 55, 56, 63.
Narration and Description   20.
Novels
    American Novels   6, 10, 12, 13, 16, 17, 18, 20, 28, 31, 34, 45, 47, 51, 54, 56, 59, 64.
    Contemporary Novels   6, 9, 18, 20, 30, 36, 44, 59.
    English Novels   1, 6, 9, 10, 12, 18, 19, 20, 30, 31, 34, 38, 40, 45, 51, 56, 59, 60, 61, 63, 64.
    French Novels   34.
    Nineteenth Century Novels   6, 26, 56.
    Spanish Novels   34.
    Survey of Novels   16.
Poetry
    General Poetry   6, 7, 12, 13, 16, 20, 42, 51, 56, 59, 61.
    Modern Poetry   6, 25, 26, 36, 44, 56, 57, 59.
    Romantic Period Poetry   20, 40, 51, 59, 60, 63.
    Seventeenth Century Poetry   20.
    Victorian Poetry   1, 10, 37, 59, 60, 63.
Short Stories   1, 4, 16, 17, 47, 52, 54, 56, 57, 58, 59, 61.
Spanish-American Literature   4, 12, 13, 21, 34, 36, 45, 51, 54, 57, 59, 63.
Themes and Characters   16.
Western World Literature   10, 21.
World Literature Survey   1, 5, 10, 16, 25, 30, 44, 45, 47, 50, 56.
MATHEMATICS
Algebra
    Abstract Algebra   45.
    Advanced Algebra   7, 18, 45, 47, 51, 52, 63.
    College Algebra   1, 3, 4, 5, 6, 7, 8, 9, 10, 11, 12, 13, 16, 17, 18, 20, 21, 22, 25, 30, 31, 32, 33, 34, 35, 36, 42, 44, 45, 46, 47, 49, 50, 51, 52, 53, 54, 55, 56, 57, 58, 59, 61, 63, 64.
    Intermediate Algebra   4, 6, 9, 12, 14, 18, 24, 25, 30, 35, 36, 44, 45, 46, 47, 55, 56, 57, 59, 62, 63.
    Linear Algebra   6, 22, 40, 47, 48, 50, 51.
    Matrix Algebra   34.
    Review Algebra   7, 22, 45, 51, 53.
Business and Finance   1, 5, 6, 16, 17, 21, 22, 25, 30, 31, 32, 34, 36, 41, 42, 45, 47, 50, 52, 56, 63.

Real Number System   55.
Statistics   1, 6, 17, 34, 36, 45, 47, 48, 50, 51, 52, 54, 56, 62, 63.
Technical Mathematics   38.
Theory of Numbers   6, 11, 45, 47, 51.
Topics in Modern Mathematics   52, 56, 63.
Trigonometry
    Plane Trigonometry   1, 3, 4, 5, 6, 7, 8, 9, 10, 11, 12, 13, 16, 17, 18, 20, 21,
        22, 30, 31, 32, 33, 34, 35, 36, 42, 44, 45, 46, 47, 48, 49, 50, 52, 53, 54,
        55, 56, 57, 59, 60, 61, 62, 63, 64.
    Spherical Trigonometry   18, 52, 63.
Vector Analysis and Potential Theory   6, 51, 52.

MUSIC

American Music   34.
Appreciation and History of Music   4, 6, 7r, 9r, 22, 31, 32, 34, 35r, 37, 45r, 55r,
    56r, 63.
Band and Orchestra   52.
Contemporary Music   34.
Counterpoint and Harmony   6, 30, 40, 52, 59.
Fundamentals of Music   4, 7, 18, 20, 64.
History of Music   7r, 22, 34, 46r.
Instrumentation   15.
Music of the East   55r.
Music's Role in Western Culture   55.
Symphonic Music   59r.
Theory of Music   34, 53, 64.

PHILOSOPHY

Aesthetics   6, 36, 45.
Buddhist Philosophy   6.
Communism   13.
Democratic American Philosophy   36.
Ethics   5, 10, 11, 13, 16, 20, 21, 30, 33, 35, 36, 38, 44, 45, 46, 50, 52.
Existentialism   10.
History of Philosophy   4, 6, 11, 13, 16, 30, 34, 45, 50, 52.
Indiàn Philosophy   37.
Individual Man   13.
Introduction to Philosophy   1, 4, 5, 6, 10, 16, 20, 21, 22, 25, 30, 31, 32, 33, 34,
    35, 36, 37, 38, 41, 44, 45, 46, 48, 52, 54, 55, 56, 57, 60.
Liberalism   6.
Logic   1, 4, 10, 13, 16, 20, 21, 22, 25, 30, 31, 32, 33, 34, 38, 40, 44, 45, 46, 48,
    49, 52, 56, 58, 63.
Medicine, Science, or Religion   13, 21, 25, 30, 33, 35, 36, 45.

Introduction to Political Science   2, 3, 5, 7, 16, 18, 19, 20, 24, 25, 27, 40, 45, 46, 55, 59.

Judicial   37.

Legislative Processes   6, 25.

Local Administration   55.

Metropolitan Areas   59.

Modern Government   61.

Municipal Government   12, 18, 20, 31, 34, 44, 45, 49, 55, 56, 59.

National Politics   1, 2, 4, 5, 6, 7, 8, 9, 10, 11, 12, 13, 15, 17, 18, 20, 21, 22, 25, 28, 30, 32, 33, 34, 35, 36, 37, 38, 41, 42, 44, 45, 46, 47, 48, 49, 50, 51, 52, 53, 54, 55, 56, 57, 59, 60, 62, 63, 64.

Parties and Politics   1, 2, 6, 16, 21, 22, 34, 37, 45, 49, 59.

Political Thought   13, 57.

Public Administration   6, 49, 50, 56.

Public Opinion   37.

State and Local Politics   1, 4, 5, 6, 9, 13, 15, 17, 18, 21, 26, 31, 33, 36, 40, 42, 44, 45, 52, 53, 55, 56, 57, 60, 62, 64.

Behavior in Politics   21.

Comparative Politics   6, 9, 11, 20, 35, 36, 44, 45, 57.

Foreign Political Science

Asian Politics   6, 57.

Chinese Politics   6, 30.

European Politics   2, 20, 22, 49, 52, 54, 56.

Far Eastern Politics   6, 30, 45.

Japanese Politics   6, 30.

Latin American Politics   6, 36, 55.

Russian Politics   20, 30, 36, 45, 56.

International Political Science

International Affairs   55.

International Politics   1, 6, 13, 16, 20, 28, 30, 31, 34, 45, 52, 53, 57, 59, 63.

United Nations and International Organizations   13, 30, 45, 52.

World Affairs   1, 4, 13, 16, 21, 28, 30, 34, 36, 49, 51, 52, 63.

Special Projects   18, 50.

Theory of Politics   12, 45.

PSYCHOLOGY

Abnormal Psychology   5, 9, 10, 12, 16, 18, 21, 28, 30, 34, 36, 41, 44, 47, 52, 60.

Adolescent Psychology   6, 7, 8, 10, 13, 17, 19, 22, 28, 30, 31, 32, 36, 38, 44, 45, 46, 47, 54, 55, 57, 63, 64.

Applied Psychology   5, 34.

Biological Basis of Behavior   35.

Business and Industrial Psychology   2, 5, 6, 9, 12, 18, 57, 61.

Real Estate Law   6, 13, 30, 44, 51.

Real Estate Principles   6, 11, 16, 22, 30, 31, 32, 37, 45, 47, 51, 53, 54, 55, 60, 64.

Tax Planning in Real Estate   6.

RECREATION (See also Physical Education)

Administration of Recreation Programs   20, 25, 30, 32, 34, 36, 42, 44, 45, 54, 55, 57, 63.

Camping   25, 30, 34.

Community Recreation   5, 7, 16, 17, 20, 28, 34, 42, 44, 55.

Crafts   55.

Family Recreation   57.

Handicapped Activities Program   42.

History and Principles of Recreation   30, 32, 34, 55, 61.

Introduction to Recreation   55.

Leadership   38.

Philosophy of Recreation   57.

Programming Recreation   16, 25, 30, 33, 37, 44, 45, 46, 55, 57, 61.

School Recreation   5, 20, 61.

Scouting   56, 57.

Social Aspects of Leisure   30.

Social Leadership   32, 55, 57.

Therapeutic Recreation   30.

Urban Recreation Organization   55.

Use of Wildlands   56.

Youth Service Organization   16.

RELIGION

Bible as Literature   1, 5, 6, 7, 44, 45, 55, 57, 58, 59, 62.

Bible Study   8, 13, 18, 34, 35, 40, 42, 45, 49, 51, 54, 57, 58.

Biblical Archaeology   63.

Christianity, Marriage, and the Family   42, 45, 57.

Church History   1, 8, 13, 57.

Comparative Religions   4, 8, 9, 13, 18, 19, 25, 31, 33, 36, 42, 47.

Contemporary Religions   13, 34, 51.

Great Religions of the World   26.

Latter-Day Saints Family   57.

Masterpieces of Sacred Literature   34.

Philosophy of Religion   34, 36.

Primitive Religions   6, 13, 20.

Problems in Religion   1.

Psychology of Religion   18, 42, 51, 57.

Religious Anthropology   6.

Teachings of Jesus   8, 13, 34, 54, 57.

TAXES
    Estate and Gift Taxes   6.
    Income Taxes   1, 6, 9, 10, 16, 22, 25, 30, 31, 33, 44, 48, 51, 53, 54, 55, 59.
    Social Security Taxes   51.
WRITING (See also Journalism)
    Business Communications
        Business Letters   1, 4, 6, 9, 12, 17, 20, 31, 32, 40, 45, 51, 54, 55, 56, 57, 63.
        Business Reports   4, 6, 9, 17, 20, 31, 40, 46, 47, 52, 55, 56, 57, 63.
        General Business Writing   2, 4, 5, 6, 9, 10, 16, 17, 20, 21, 22, 25, 32, 35, 37, 40, 45, 46, 47, 48, 51, 52, 55, 56, 57, 61, 63.
        Technical Writing   2, 6, 7, 9, 18, 20, 46, 47, 55, 56, 59, 63.
    College Writing   28.
    Creative Writing   6, 7, 16, 20, 30, 31, 32, 34, 40, 42, 44, 45, 46, 56, 57, 58, 63.
    Expository Writing   16, 17, 18, 20, 26, 30, 34, 35, 37, 45, 52, 56, 59, 63.
    Feature Magazine Articles   5, 9, 15, 16, 20, 21, 22, 30, 35, 36, 44, 45, 47, 51, 53, 55, 57, 63.
    Fiction Writing   18, 38, 45, 51, 56, 57, 59.
    Playwriting   22, 30, 40, 45, 55.
    Poetry Writing   32, 38, 56, 57, 59, 61.
    Radio and Television Writing   17, 22, 30, 45, 51.
    Science and Engineering Writing   6, 18, 22, 59.
    Speech Writing   5, 22, 42.
    Story Writing   2, 4, 10, 12, 18, 30, 31, 32, 35, 37, 40, 45, 46, 47, 51, 52, 56, 59, 63.

6

College Level Courses—Graduate Credit

Most colleges and universities in the United States grant graduate credit for on-campus or in-residence study only. Recognition is, however, growing for the role correspondence study can play in graduate programs. Some accredited schools have started a new trend in this important direction by offering correspondence study courses for graduate credit to those students who qualify.

The courses listed in this chapter are available at the present time. Refer to Part II, Chapter 3, for the names and addresses of the institutions which correspond to the numbers following each course offering noted below.

GRADUATE CREDIT COURSES

ACCOUNTING
  Cost   34.
AGRICULTURE
  Fruit   34.
  Insect Control   34.
ANTHROPOLOGY
  Cultural   34.
ART
  Drawing and Painting   18.
BUSINESS
  Business Administration
    Administration Policy   35.
    Human Behavior   35.
  Finance
    Investments and Securities   34.
  Insurance
    Introduction, General Principles   18.
    Property, Casualty, etc.   18.
  Law
    Business Law   19.
  Management and Organization
    Business   35.
    Human Relations   35.
    Job Analysis   35.
    Personnel Selection   18, 35.
  Marketing
    Institutions   18.
    Promotion   18.
    Retailing   18.
ECONOMICS
  History of American Economics   34.
  Labor Movements   18.
  Social Insurance   34.
EDUCATION
  Administration
    General Administration   34.
    Junior College Administration   18.
  Alcohol   18.
  Audio-Visual Techniques   18, 45.

Child and Society   18.
Childhood   18.
Curriculum Planning   34.
Distributive Education   18, 19.
General Survey of Education Today   18.
Guidance   18.
Historical Foundations of Education   38.
History of Education   18, 19.
Industrial Education   18, 19.
Philosophical Foundations of Education   38.
Philosophy of Education   18.
Psychology of Education   18.
Special Education   18.
Statistics of Education   18, 19, 34.
Tests and Measurements   18, 19.
Vocational Education   18, 19.

EDUCATIONAL METHODS
Early Childhood   18.
Elementary Education
    Arithmetic   18.
    General   18.
    Health   18.
    Language Arts   18.
    Modern Mathematics   19.
    Physical Education   18.
    Reading Skills   18.
    Science   18, 19.
    Social Studies   18, 19.
    Spanish   20.
High School or Secondary Education
    English   18.
    General   18.
    Health   18.
    Journalism for Teachers   34.
    Physical Education   18.
    Reading Skills   18.
Literacy Education
    Pre-School   18.
ENGINEERING
Advanced Drawing and Drafting   18.
Mechanics   34.

ENGLISH
    Composition and Grammar for Teachers   18.
    Syntax   19r.
GEOGRAPHY
    Conservation and Natural Resources   34.
    Economic Geography   18.
    Manufacturing and Commerce   18.
    Political Geography   19.
    United States and Canada   18.
    Urban Geography   18.
HISTORY
    African History   19.
    American History
        Colonial History   18, 34.
        Diplomatic History   18, 19, 34.
        Recent History   18, 34.
        Revolutionary History   34.
        Southern History   18, 34.
        Twentieth Century History   19, 34.
        United States History   18.
    English History   34.
    European History
        Medieval History   18, 19.
        Reformation History   34.
        Renaissance History   34.
    French History   34.
    German History   34.
    Russian History   34.
    States History   19.
HOME ECONOMICS
    Nutrition   18.
LANGUAGES
    Beginning French   24.
    Beginning German   24.
    Greek Grammar   18.
    Spanish
        Beginning Spanish   34.
        Reading Spanish   34.
    Spanish-American Literature   34.
LITERATURE
    American Literature

SPEECH
　　Pathology of Speech　　18.
WRITING
　　Fictional Writing　　18.
　　Short Story Writing　　18.

7

College Certificate Programs

In addition to general non-credit courses offered by colleges and universities in Chapter 8, a number of schools have designed special certificate programs. These areas of study are geared to meet specific professional goals or vocational goals. They concentrate in a particular field of interest. A wide range of subject matter is covered. The programs are suitable for individuals with widely varying educational backgrounds.

On suitable completion of the special course sequence, a certificate of recognition is awarded the student. This certificate indicates his or her proficiency and achievement.

Refer to Part II, Chapter 3, for the names and addresses of the institutions which correspond to the numbers following each certificate program offering noted below.

COLLEGE CERTIFICATE PROGRAMS

ACCOUNTING
    General Accounting   6, 51, 63.
    Hospital Accounting   16.
AGRICULTURE
    Agricultural Entomology   60.
    General Agriculture   30.
BUSINESS
    Business Administration   6, 51, 63.
    Data Processing   30, 47.
    Industrial Relations   6.
    Insurance   9.
    Investments   30.
    Organization and Management   30.
    Personnel Management   24, 30.
    Supervision   30.
    Transportation   51.
CHILDREN'S BOOKS   30.
CITIZENSHIP   55.
CITY PLANNING
    City and Regional Planning   6.
    Public Administration   30.
DENTAL
    Dental Assistant   40.
    Dental Technology   40.
DIGITAL COMPUTERS
    Computer Concepts   55.
    Digital Computers and Programming   30, 55.
    Introduction to Computer Programming   30, 55.
    Introduction to Digital Computers   30, 55.
    Programming (FORTRAN)   55.
EDUCATION
    Childhood   7.
ENGINEERING
    Civil   51.
    Drawing and Design   30, 55.
    Electrical Engineering   30, 51.
    Electron Microscopy   30.
    General Engineering   63.
    Power Plant Engineering   30.

8

College Non-Credit Courses

Many colleges and universities throughout the United States offer abundant non-credit courses through correspondence. These study programs are geared for those students who are not concerned about receiving college credit for the courses they take. They are for those wanting cultural enlightenment and professional learning instead.

All 64 NUEA institutions will allow enrollments in any of their credit courses on a non-credit basis. These courses are completely covered in Chapters 4, 5, and 6.

Many of the courses listed below are designed to give specific instruction in areas of study not normally covered in the regular curriculum. Refer to Part II, Chapter 3, for the names and addresses of the institutions which correspond to the numbers following each course offering noted below.

COLLEGE NON-CREDIT COURSES

PART IV

9

Glossary of Terms

ACADEMIC YEAR: The period of time from the beginning of the first semester or quarter in September to the close of the second semester or fourth quarter in June.

ACCREDITATION: The type of recognition held by an educational institution. There are a number of nationally recognized accrediting agencies and associations which are reliable authorities on the quality of training offered by educational institutions. By voluntarily conforming to the standards of excellence set by an agency or association, an institution becomes eligible for inclusion in its accredited or approved list.

ADMISSION: Acceptance of an applicant for enrollment.

ASSOCIATE DEGREE: Recognition of successful completion of one of the prescribed two-year programs of study.

BACHELOR'S DEGREE: The degree granted after successful completion of an approved undergraduate college or university program.

CLASS: The regularly scheduled meeting of an academic course, or a group of students whose graduation date is the same—freshman, sophmore, junior, senior.

CLASSIFICATION: The designation used for the student's year of study in terms of his progress toward his chosen degree—freshman, sophomore, junior, senior.

COLLEGE: An organizational unit of the university normally offering courses and curricula leading to a particular degree or degrees, and supervising the academic progress of students working toward those degrees. The degree colleges to which students may transfer, if eligible, after completion of the freshman year are: Arts and Sciences, Business Administration, Education, Engineering, Fine Arts, Nursing, etc. The Graduate School, the School of Law, and the School of Medicine, etc., offer advanced study.

COURSE: A particular subject being studied—thus, a course in English.

CREDIT: A unit of credit, semester or quarter hour, represents approximately one class period or hour a week (for which outside preparation is required) for one academic term.

CURRICULUM: A body of courses required for a degree or a diploma, or constituting

74

a major field of study. A program of study consisting of required courses, a major, minors, and electives.

DEGREE: A title bestowed as official recognition for the completion of a curriculum. It is simply formal recognition that a student has satisfactorily completed a prescribed course of study. The bachelor's degree is the first-level degree granted normally upon completion of a four-year course of study in a given field. The Bachelor of Laws degree, however, is a professional degree and normally requires seven years of college study. The master's degree is an advanced degree ranking above the bachelor's degree and below the doctorate. It normally requires at least one year beyond the bachelor's degree. The doctor's degree, or doctorate, is an advanced degree requiring at least three years beyond the bachelor's degree. The honorary degree is bestowed in recognition of outstanding merit or achievement without reference to the fulfillment of academic course requirements. Abbreviations used are: BA—Bachelor of Arts; BAE—Bachelor of Art Education; B Arch. E—Bachelor of Architectural Engineering; B Arch.—Bachelor of Architecture; BFA—Bachelor of Fine Arts; BM—Bachelor of Music; BME—Bachelor of Music Education; BS—Bachelor of Science; MA—Master of Arts; MS—Master of Science; DVM—Doctor of Veterinary Medicine; Ed D—Doctor of Education; Ph D—Doctor of Philosophy.

DEPARTMENT: A division of the college or university which offers instruction in a particular branch of knowledge. The Department of Music is one example.

ELECTIVES: That part of a student's program which he selects according to his special interests, supplementing a program of required subjects. A course which the student may study by choice but which may or may not be required for his particular degree.

EXTRACURRICULAR ACTIVITIES: Nonacademic student activities, such as debating, dramatics, athletics, student clubs, publications, etc.

GRADUATE STUDENT: One who has earned a bachelor's degree and is enrolled for advanced work in the Graduate School.

MAJOR: The field in which the student's studies are primarily concentrated. A major includes the required basic or elementary work of the first two years of study in a certain field, plus a specific number of semester or quarter hours of advanced work during the junior and senior years in that same field.

MINOR: A field of concentration but of a lesser degree than a major field. A minor usually consists of 16 semester credit hours of advanced work in a particular field. A secondary subject of study in one field of learning.

NEW STUDENT: One who is registering for the first time in the university or college, or a student transferring from non-degree to degree status in the school.

NUMBERING SYSTEM: All courses are numbered in terms of three digits. The first digit indicates the class year in which the subject ordinarily is taken; the last digit indicates the credit hours and all three serve to denote the course. For example, a course numbered 123 should be interpreted as a freshman course carrying three hours of credit.

PRE-PROFESSIONAL PROGRAM: A program of studies designed to prepare a student for entrance to a professional school—e.g., pre-law, pre-medical, etc.

PREREQUISITE: A course or courses that a student must complete before being allowed to take a more advanced course. The requirement which must be met before a certain course can be taken for credit.

READMITTED STUDENT: One who has previously registered for residence credit in the college or university but whose attendance has been interrupted by one or more semesters.

REGISTRATION: The act of enrolling in classes. A registration period is held at the beginning of each semester and summer session. At that time, the student with the help of his adviser chooses a program of courses for the session and fills in forms necessary for the proper recording of his enrollment.

REQUIRED COURSES: Courses specified by the faculty which all degree candidates must satisfactorily complete.

RESIDENT STUDY: Enrollment in courses on the campus or in courses off-campus which are allowed by special action to count as residence credit, as distinguished from correspondence or extension credit.

RETURNING STUDENT: One who was registered in the immediately preceding session.

SCHEDULE: A listing of courses you are taking each semester.

SEMESTER OR QUARTER CREDIT HOUR: A measure of credit given for courses successfully completed. Credit hours are based on the number of clock hours a class meets each week for a quarter or a semester. The equivalency ratios of semester and quarter hours are:

Semester Hours		*Quarter Hours*
1⅓	=	2
2	=	3
2⅔	=	4
3	=	4½
3⅓	=	5

TRANSFER CREDIT: Credit toward a degree granted by a college or university for work satisfactorily completed elsewhere.

TRIAL STUDY: Tentative schedule of courses to be taken in the coming quarter or semester.

TUITION: The fee paid by the student for instruction.

UNDERGRADUATE: A student who is working for a bachelor's (baccalaureate) degree. The first four years of a college education.

Bibliography

Bern, H.A. "Open, then, a Door," *Phi Delta Kappan*, Vol. 51, No. 6, February, 1970.

Bittner, W.S. and H.F. Mallory. *University Teaching by Mail*. New York: MacMillan Company, 1933.

Brandenburg Memorial Essays on Correspondence Instruction. Vol. 1 and 2. Madison, Wisconsin: University of Wisconsin, 1966.

Carey, J.T. *Forms and Forces in University Adult Education*. Brookline, Massachusetts: CSLEA, 1961.

Childs, Gayle B. *An Annotated Bibliography of Correspondence Study*. Lincoln, Nebraska: University of Nebraska, 1960.

Correspondence Definitions. Bloomington, Indiana: Indiana University Press, 1951.

Correspondence Education, a Bibliography. Washington, D.C.: Marine Corps Institute, 1959.

Erdos, Renee. *Teaching by Correspondence*. London: Longmans, 1967.

Experiments in Correspondence Study. Madison, Wisconsin: University of Wisconsin Press, 1955.

Graff, Kurt. "Correspondence Instruction in the History of the Western World," *Home Study Review*, Vol. 8, No. 1, 1967.

Grumman, R.M. *University Extension in Action*. Chapel Hill, North Carolina: University of North Carolina Press, 1946.

Houle, C.O. *The Inquiring Mind*. Madison, Wisconsin: University of Wisconsin Press, 1961.

Hughes, R.M. *Education—America's Magic*. Ames, Iowa: Iowa State University Press, 1946.

Kelly, T. *A History of Adult Education in Great Britain*. Liverpool: Liverpool University Press, 1962.

Lovejoy, C.E. *Lovejoy's Complete Guide to American Colleges and Universities*. New York: Simon & Shuster, 1970.

MacKenzie, O. and others. *Correspondence Instruction in the United States*. New York: McGraw-Hill, 1968.

Morton, John, R. *University Extension in the United States*. University, Alabama: University of Alabama Press, 1953.

Noffsinger, J.S. *Correspondence Schools*. New York: MacMillan Company, 1926.

78

Potter, G.R. *Planning and Writing Correspondence Courses*. Berkeley, California: University of California Press, 1946.

_____. *Taking a Correspondence Course: A Manual for Students*. Berkeley, California: University of California Press, 1949.

Reid, R.H. *American Degree Mills*. Washington, D.C.: American Council on Education, 1959.

"Supervised Correspondence Instruction in the Secondary School," *The Bulletin of the National Association of Secondary School Principals*, Vol. 36, December, 1952.

Wedemeyer, C.A., and G.B. Childs. *New Perspectives in University Correspondence Study*. Chicago: Center for the Liberal Education of Adults, 1961.

Wierman, A.E. *The Mechanics of Correspondence Instruction*. Englewood Cliffs, New Jersey: Prentice-Hall, 1947.

Wyrich, R. *Ten Million Alumni*. Washington, D.C.: National Home Study Council, 1968.

Yang, C. *Meet the U.S.A. Handbook for Foreign Students in the United States*. New York: Institute of International Education, 1947.

NOTE: The correspondence bulletins (catalogs) of each college and university listed in Chapter 3 were also utilized in compiling the detailed course data contained in this handbook.

FOR FURTHER STUDY

The following ARCO BOOKS may be just what you need at this time for the extra help that will assure your success in the college career you have chosen. They can be the most important books you will ever buy.

Scholastic Aptitude Tests

Arco Editorial Board

Complete preparation for all sections of the Scholastic Aptitude Test now available in the most authoritative, comprehensive book ever published. Thousands of questions and answers similar to the ones students encounter on the test—opposites, sentence completion, word list, verbal analogies, reading comprehension, vocabulary, grammar and correct English usage, fractions, decimals, percents, interest, algebra and more. Model examinations for the S.A.T. achievement tests in French, German, English composition, Latin and Spanish are provided as well as full details of the College Entrance Examination Boards.

L/C No. 67-29067
© 1969
7-7/8" x 10-1/4"; 480 pages

ISBN 0-668-02039-3	LR cloth: $6.50
ISBN 0-668-02038-5	paper: $4.00

How to Prepare Your College Application

Kussin, Louis
Kussin, Steven

An indispensable guide for all high school students who are looking ahead to college, for parents, and for school guidance counselors. This book explains in detail how to fill out the all-important college application and analyses the different types of essay questions asked by various schools. To help you write the best possible essay, hundreds of sample answers have been included. A list of colleges shows at a glance which of the fifty types of application form is used by a particular college, and one extremely important chapter tells how you may still gain acceptance by a college even though you have been rejected by all the schools to which you applied. The special section dealing with financial aid tells what scholarships are available, how to apply for loans and other types of aid, and how and where to get help. A Parents' Financial Statement is analyzed in detail, and a filled-out sample shows how to avoid various pitfalls.

"An invaluable aid both to students who are about to apply for admittance to college and to school guidance counselors."—New Books for Teenagers. *"Should be in the hands of every high school student before he writes his first letter of application to any college."*—The World of Books. *"The Kussins present a treasury to the student who is overwhelmed."*—Catholic Educational Review.

L/C No. 65-28109
© 1965
7-7/8" x 10-1/4"; 224 pages

ISBN 0-668-01310-9	paper: $3.00

Taking Tests and Scoring High

Honig, Fred

Includes a unique, detailed, step-by-step analysis of every type and form of test question any examinee is likely to encounter as well as suggestions and tips on how to answer each question correctly. This thorough book also contains techniques, procedures, and guidelines for studying and learning in general; complete descriptions and explanations of test procedures; and methods for concentrating one's study for a specific test. Not only will this book prove invaluable for anyone preparing for a civil service exam, high school or college test, college entrance or scholarship exam, employment or promotion test, but also for self-help organizations.

"The material contained would be useful in almost any kind of examination . . . Mr. Honig provides many examples of the kind of questions that are so often pitfalls of the unwary test-taker."—Publisher's Weekly. *"Successful learning—the RIGHT WAY to study—must be mastered if you want to get the most out of your studies. This book gives you suggestions, guidelines, and procedures."*—American News of Books. *"The book should be a useful tool for those organizations helping clients from disadvantaged areas gain test-taking sophistication."*—Vocational Advisory Service.

L/C No. 67-14971
© 1967
7-7/8" x 10-1/4"; 144 pages

ISBN 0-668-01348-6	LR cloth: $5.00
ISBN 0-668-01347-8	paper: $3.00

College Scholarships

ARCO Editorial Board

A thorough guide to all the most important scholarships now being offered by colleges and universities, government agencies, and private organizations. This book includes a directory of almost two thousand institutions of higher learning and basic information about each one, a realistic sample exam based on ones actually given to scholarship candidates, information about the various types of scholarships and grants, and study sections on every subject included on the exams.

L/C No. 66-17179
© 1966
7-7/8" x 10-1/4"; 375 pages

ISBN 0-668-00569-6	paper: $4.00

(continued)

Triple Your Reading Speed

Cutler, Dr. Wade E.

The famous Cutler Accele*read* Method—a tested, proven way to dramatically increase reading speed while actually improving comprehension. Until now, speed reading was only taught in schools—often expensive, time-consuming, and inconvenient. Now, anyone can triple his reading speed at home, at his leisure, with the study course complete in this book. Since 1965 the Cutler Accele*read* Method has been taught with great success to 10,000 students and adults. Upon completion of the course each of these people showed impressive improvement in his individual reading rate and comprehension score. Here then, for the first time, are these famous study and practice exercises in easy-to-follow-and-use book form. Before beginning, the potential speed reader measures his reading rate in a special test. He then learns how to identify and overcome his particular blocks to better reading: vocalization, sub-vocalization, wasted eye movements, eye fatigue. New techniques presented include previewing, pacing and block reading, the two-stop method and exercises for expanding peripheral vision. Closing sections show how to prepare for and score high on various kinds of comprehension tests.

"For those who'd like to take a rapid reading course, yet don't have enough time to attend classes, this book will be helpful."—Journal of Extension.

L/C No. 70-93503
© 1970
7-7/8" x 10-1/4"; 192 pages

ISBN 0-668-02084-9	LR cloth: $5.00
ISBN 0-668-02083-0	paper: $3.00

How to Write Reports, Papers, Theses, Articles   Riebel, John P.

The ability to express ideas in writing and in speaking heads the list of requirements for sucess. According to Professor Riebel, one does not need a degree in english or journalism to write a good paper. Observing a few simple rules and applying common sense will enable anyone to put ideas on paper with minimum effort and maximum impact. Included in this handbook are all the elements of good writing; a composition guide consisting of a review of the important principles of grammar and punctuation, a list of words frequently misspelled, a glossary of words and phrases often misused and confused, accepted standard abbreviations, an outline of the principles of modern business letter writing and a guide to the types of business letters technical students should know how to write.

© 1971
8-1/2" x 11"; 128 pages

ISBN 0-668-02392-9	LR cloth: $8.00
ISBN 0-668-02391-0	paper: $5.00

Scoring High on College Entrance Tests

Turner, David

Here is a most complete and authoratative study manual to prepare a student for every possible type of college entrance examination he may have to take—including the College Boards, the General Educational Development Tests, The American Council on Education Psychological Examination, and the Engineering and Physical Science Aptitude Test. Thousands of sample questions patterned after actual exams—with answer keys—cover math, vocabulary, English usage, reading comprehension, mechanical insight, spatial relations, graph interpretation, and non-verbal reasoning. Proven study methods for scoring high are clearly set forth so that this wealth of material may be used to best advantage. Answer sheets (computer-scored type) are provided to give the student valuable practice in test-taking techniques. A ten-thousand-word vocabulary list compiled from past examinations, plus hundreds of word etymologies, will help raise the student's score by increasing his command of the English language. Copies of actual forms used by interviewers from big-name schools give the applicant a good idea of the qualities admissions personnel look for. This book will arm the student with greater knowledge and increased self-confidence to enter the growing competition for the limited college space, available.

"Counselors will find it a valuable source of information in advising college entrants." — **Mental Measurements Yearbook**

L/C No. 68-57161
© 1968   7-7/8" x 10-1/4"; 638 pages

ISBN 0-668-01859-3	LR cloth: $6.50
ISBN 0-668-01858-5	paper: $4.00

Miller Analogies Test—1400 Analogy Questions

For the student preparing for college or graduate school entrance examinations containing word-analogy questions; recommended for the guidance counselor's library. This programmed book works as a teaching machine, arranged to give the student immediate reinforcement of each idea learned. In the first section the word analogies are grouped according to kinds of relationships: purpose relationship, cause and effect, part to whole, part to part, action to object, synonym relationship, characteristic relationship, sequence relationship, grammatical relationship, numerical relationship, association relationship. Sample tests, in which different types of types of analogy questions are combined at random, are given in the second section.

L/C No. 67-21844
© 1967; second edition
7-7/8" x 10-1/4"; 160 pages

ISBN 0-668-01115-7	LR cloth: $6.50
ISBN 0-668-01114-9	paper: $4.00